DEC   2014

MEDITERRANEAN ART

FUN AND EASY ART FROM AROUND THE WORLD

ALEX KUSKOWSKI

Super Sandcastle

An Imprint of Abdo Publishing
www.abdopublishing.com

Consulting Editor, Diane Craig,
M.A./Reading Specialist

VISIT US AT WWW.ABDOPUBLISHING.COM

Published by Abdo Publishing, a division of ABDO, PO Box 398166, Minneapolis, Minnesota 55439. Copyright © 2015 by Abdo Consulting Group, Inc. International copyrights reserved in all countries. No part of this book may be reproduced in any form without written permission from the publisher. Super SandCastle™ is a trademark and logo of Abdo Publishing.

Printed in the United States of America, North Mankato, Minnesota
062014
092014

THIS BOOK CONTAINS RECYCLED MATERIALS

Editor: Liz Salzmann
Content Developer: Nancy Tuminelly
Cover and Interior Design and Production: Mighty Media, Inc.
Photo Credits: Jen Schoeller, Shutterstock

The following manufacturers/names appearing in this book are trademarks: Crayola®, Elmer's® Glue-All™, UL®, Lactaid®, Scribbles®, Celebrate It®, Barbasol®, Crystal Sugar®, Sharpie®

Library of Congress Cataloging-in-Publication Data
Kuskowski, Alex., author.
 Super simple Mediterranean art : fun and easy art from around the world / Alex Kuskowski ; consulting editor, Diane Craig, M.A., reading specialist.
   pages cm. -- (Super simple cultural art)
 Audience: Ages 5-10.
  ISBN 978-1-62403-282-0
1. Handicraft--Juvenile literature. 2. Mediterranean Region--Civilization--Miscellanea--Juvenile literature. I. Craig, Diane, editor. II. Title. III. Series: Super simple cultural art.
 TT160.K87435 2015
 745.509182'2--dc23
                    2013043460

Super SandCastle™ books are created by a team of professional educators, reading specialists, and content developers around five essential components—phonemic awareness, phonics, vocabulary, text comprehension, and fluency—to assist young readers as they develop reading skills and strategies and increase their general knowledge. All books are written, reviewed, and leveled for guided reading, early reading intervention, and Accelerated Reader® programs for use in shared, guided, and independent reading and writing activities to support a balanced approach to literacy instruction.

TO ADULT HELPERS

Children can have a lot of fun learning about different cultures through arts and crafts. Be sure to supervise them as they work on the projects in this book. Let the kids do as much as possible on their own. But be ready to step in and help if necessary. Also, kids may be using glue, paint, markers, and clay. Make sure they protect their clothes and work surfaces.

KEY SYMBOL

In this book, you may see this symbol. Here is what it means.

HOT!
You will be working with something hot. Get help.

TABLE OF CONTENTS

GELATO

Gelato is the Italian word for a soft, thick kind of ice cream. People eat gelato for a sweet snack.

COOL CULTURE

Get ready to go on a **cultural** art adventure! All around the world, people make art. They use art to show different **traditions** and ideas. Learning about different cultures with art can be a lot of fun.

The Mediterranean is a region. It is made up of countries that are around the Mediterranean Sea. Countries such as Greece, Italy, and Turkey are all part of the Mediterranean region. People in this region have shared ideas with each other since ancient times.

Mediterranean Sea

BEFORE YOU START

Remember to treat other people and **cultures** with respect. Respect their art, **jewelry**, and clothes too. These things can have special meaning to people.

There are a few rules for doing art projects:

▶ **PERMISSION**
Make sure to get **permission** to do a project. You might want to use things you find around the house. Ask first!

▶ **SAFETY**
Get help from an adult when using something hot or sharp. Never use a stove or oven by yourself.

ART IN MEDITERRANEAN CULTURE

People in the Mediterranean region create many beautiful things. Some are for everyday use. Others are for special occasions. The **designs** in Mediterranean art often have special meanings.

 The first real plays were performed in ancient Greece. The actors wore **masks** to present their characters.

 The **fez** is a hat from the **Ottoman Empire**. Fezzes are often worn in eastern Mediterranean countries.

 People in Turkey have made **marbled paper** for more than 400 years. In Europe, it is sometimes called "Turkish paper."

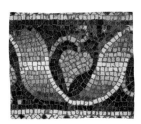 **Mosaics** are pictures made of pieces of glass or stone. Mosaics from 2,700 years ago have been found in Turkey!

 In ancient Greece, people often decorated **vases**. They painted patterns and pictures on the vases.

 The ancient Greeks held a **competition** every four years. The **Olympic Games** are still held today.

 **Scrolls** are ancient books. Ancient Greeks, Egyptians, and Romans all used scrolls.

 The **Italian flag** is green, white, and red. Some people say that the colors represent hope, faith, and charity.

WHAT YOU NEED

acrylic paint, paintbrush & foam brush

air-dry clay

aluminum foil & waxed paper

aluminum tray & baking sheet

black tassel

black tea bag

cardboard & card stock paper

craft glue, hot glue gun & glue sticks

craft sticks, wooden skewer & wooden dowels

felt

food coloring

fork

glass vase

jewels

key chain ring

magnetic strips

marker & pencil

measuring cups

mixing bowls &
mixing spoon

newspaper

paper cups &
paper plates

pint size ice cream
container

puffy paint

red pom-pom

ribbon

ruler

scissors

shaving cream

sponge

strawberries

Styrofoam ball

sugar

tape

tissue paper &
colored paper

white chocolate
chips

wire hanger

wooden candle
cups

PAINTED VASE RELIC

Make your own ancient vase!

WHAT YOU NEED

newspaper

glass vase

black and terra-cotta acrylic paint

paintbrush

air-dry clay

hot glue gun and glue sticks

DIRECTIONS

1   Cover your work area with newspaper. Paint the glass vase with a coat of black paint. Let it dry. Paint it with another coat of black paint. Let it dry.

② Paint a pattern around the middle of the vase with terra-cotta paint. Let it dry.

3   Roll out two snakes of air-dry clay. Bend them into curvy handles for the vase. Let the clay dry according to the directions on the package.

④ Paint the handles black. Let the paint dry.

⑤ Have an adult help you hot glue the handles to the vase. Glue the handles opposite each other.

MINI RED FEZ

Wear a Turkish hat to your next party!

WHAT YOU NEED

clean, pint-size ice cream container

scissors

red & black felt

marker

craft glue

ruler

hot glue gun and glue sticks

black tassel

DIRECTIONS

1. Trace the bottom of the container on the red felt. Trace around the edge. Cut out the circle.

2. Glue the circle to the bottom of the container.

3. Wrap red felt around the container. Cut the felt to fit around the container. The edges of the felt should **overlap** slightly. Glue the felt to the container. Let the glue dry.

4. Cut a circle of black felt 1 inch (2.5 cm) across. Have an adult help you put a dot of hot glue on the hat. Put the end of the tassel's string in the glue. Press the felt circle on top. Let the glue dry.

QUICK TIP: Add a chin **strap** to hold your fez on. Cut a piece of black elastic. Use hot glue to **attach** the ends inside the hat on opposite sides.

MAKE IT MARBLED

Wrap it up in cool marbled paper!

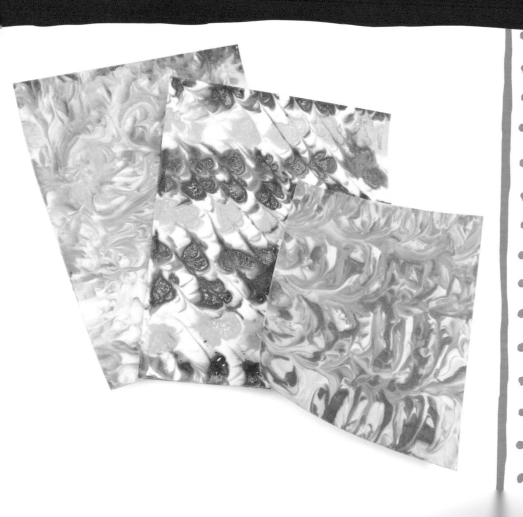

WHAT YOU NEED

newspaper

aluminum tray

shaving cream

cardboard

food coloring

wooden skewer

card stock paper

DIRECTIONS

1. Cover your work area with newspaper. Fill the bottom of the aluminum tray with 1 inch (2.5 cm) of shaving cream. Smooth the cream with a piece of cardboard.

2. Put drops of food coloring on the shaving cream. **Swirl** them around with the wooden skewer.

3. Lay a piece of card stock on top of the shaving cream. Press down lightly.

4. Carefully lift the card stock. Lay it face up on newspaper. Use cardboard to scrape the shaving cream off of the card stock. Let it dry.

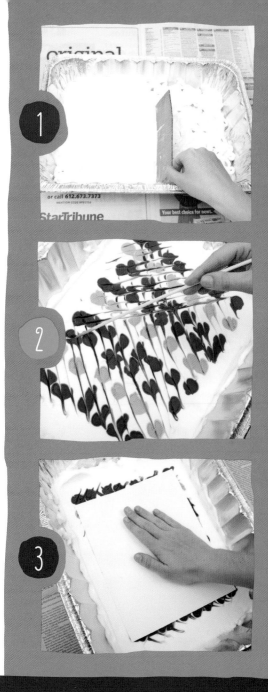

OLYMPIC GAMES FUN

Have your own games and award prizes!

WHAT YOU NEED

air-dry clay

ruler

key chain ring

puffy paint

gold acrylic paint

paintbrush

ribbon

paper

tape

small paper cup

aluminum foil

craft glue

red, orange, and yellow tissue paper

DIRECTIONS

1. Make a disk out of clay. Make it ½ inch (1.3 cm) thick and 3 inches (7.6 cm) wide.

2. Press the key chain ring into the clay. Leave half of the ring outside the clay. Form the disk around the ring. Let the clay dry according to the directions on the package.

3. Write "Gold Medal" on the disk with puffy paint. Let the paint dry.

PROJECT CONTINUES ON THE NEXT PAGE

DIRECTIONS (CONTINUED)

(4) Paint the disk gold. Let the paint dry.

(5) Cut 16 inches (40.6 cm) of ribbon. Thread it through the key chain ring. Tie the ends of the ribbon together.

(6) Roll a piece of colored paper into a tube. Widen one end to make a cone. Make sure it's wide enough for the paper cup to fit inside it. Tape the paper so it won't unroll.

DIRECTIONS (CONTINUED)

7. Put the paper cup in the cone. Tape the cone and paper cup together.

8. Cover the cone and cup with aluminum foil. Glue it in place. Let the glue dry.

9. **Crumple** red, orange, and yellow tissue paper together. Make it look like a flame.

10. Put glue in the bottom of the cup. Press the tissue paper flame to the glue. Hold it there for a minute until it stays. Let the glue dry.

MOSAIC FRAME

Make a fun mosaic!

WHAT YOU need

colored card stock paper

scissors

ruler

8 craft sticks

black acrylic paint

paintbrush

craft glue

magnetic strips

DIRECTIONS

1. Cut yellow, green, and orange card stock into pieces that are about ½ inch (1.3 cm) square.

2. Cut the rounded ends off of the craft sticks. Paint them black. Let the paint dry.

3. Lay two sticks side by side. Lay another two sticks about 2½ inches (6.3 cm) from the first two sticks.

4. Put glue on one end of the craft sticks. Lay two craft sticks on top of the glue. Glue the last two craft sticks across the other end the same way. Let the glue dry .

5. Arrange the card stock squares in a pattern on the frame. Glue them in place. Let the glue dry. Stick magnetic strips to the back of the frame.

GET YOUR GELATO

Scoop up this craft!

WHAT YOU NEED

newspaper

paper cup

acrylic paint

paintbrush

Styrofoam ball

craft glue

red pom-pom

DIRECTIONS

1   Cover your work area with newspaper. Paint the paper cup dark brown. Let the paint dry. Add a second coat of paint. Let it dry.

(2)   Paint a light brown crisscross pattern on the cup. Make it look like an ice cream cone.

(3)   Paint the Styrofoam ball green. Let the paint dry. Add brown marks. Let it dry.

(4)   Glue the ball to the top of the cup. Glue the pom-pom on top of the ball. Let the glue dry.

ACTING OUT MASKS

Get caught up in theater!

WHAT YOU NEED

2 paper plates

pencil

scissors

newspaper

acrylic paint

paintbrush

2 craft sticks

tape

DIRECTIONS

1   Hold a paper plate to your face. Have a helper mark where your eyes and mouth are. Repeat with the second plate. Draw a smiling mouth on one plate. Draw a frowning mouth on the other plate. Draw ovals for eyes on both plates.

(2) Cut out the mouths and eyes.

3   Cover your work area with newspaper. Paint the plates different colors. Paint the craft sticks. Let the paint dry.

(4) Add eyebrows and other **details**. Dip a pencil eraser in paint to make dots around the edges of the plates.

(5) Cut a slot in each plate under the mouths. Slide a craft stick into each slot. Tape the sticks to the backs of the plates.

ROMAN SCROLL

Roll up the written word!

WHAT YOU NEED

newspaper	measuring cup
2 wooden dowels, 12 inches (30.5 cm) long	2 sheets of plain paper, 11 x 17 inches (28 x 43 cm)
4 wooden candle cups	sponge
hot glue gun and glue sticks	2 wire hangers
brown acrylic paint	craft glue
foam brush	ribbon
jewels	ruler
3 black tea bags	scissors

DIRECTIONS

1. Cover your work area with newspaper. Have an adult help you hot glue a candle cup to each end of both dowels. Let the glue dry.

2. Paint both dowels brown. Let the paint dry.

3. Glue a **jewel** to each end of both dowels. Let the glue dry.

PROJECT CONTINUES ON THE NEXT PAGE

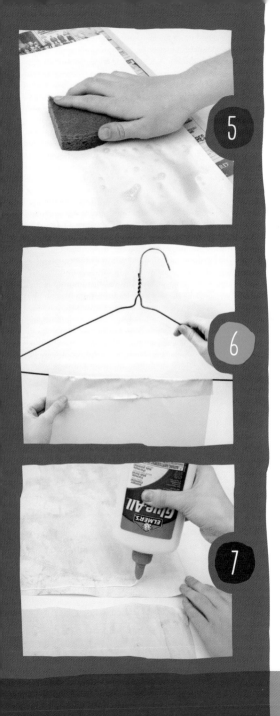

DIRECTIONS (CONTINUED)

4   Put three black tea bags into 1 cup of hot water. Let them sit 10 minutes.

5   Lay two sheets of plain paper on the newspaper. Dip the sponge in the tea water. Drag the sponge over the sheets of paper. Cover them with tea water.

6   Put the end of each sheet of paper over a hanger. Hang them up to dry.

7   Glue a short edge of one sheet to a short edge of the other sheet. Let the glue dry.

DIRECTIONS (CONTINUED)

8. Put a line of glue along the length of one dowel. Glue a short edge of the paper to the dowel. Glue the opposite edge of the paper to the other dowel the same way. Let the glue dry.

9. Roll the dowels toward each other. Make sure the paper wraps around the dowels as you roll them. Keep going until the dowels meet in the middle.

10. Tie a ribbon around the scroll.

SWEET ITALIAN SNACK

Chow down on the colors of the Italian flag!

WHAT YOU NEED

baking sheet

waxed paper

measuring cups

½ cup sugar

green food coloring

mixing bowls

fork

1 cup white chocolate chips

mixing spoon

2 cups strawberries

DIRECTIONS

1 Cover the baking sheet with waxed paper.

2 Put the sugar and 8 drops of food coloring in a bowl. Mix with a fork.

3 Put the white chocolate chips in a bowl. Microwave it for 30 seconds. Stir the chocolate. Keep heating and stirring until the chocolate is melted.

4 Dip two thirds of a strawberry in the white chocolate.

5 Dip one third of the strawberry in the sugar mixture. Place it on the baking sheet.

6 Repeat steps 4 and 5 with all of the strawberries. Refrigerate for 10 minutes.

GLOSSARY

attach – to join or connect.

competition – a game or contest.

crumple – to crush or bend something out of shape.

culture – the ideas, art, and other products of a particular group of people.

design – a decorative pattern or arrangement.

detail – a small part of something.

jewel – a precious stone such as an emerald or a diamond.

jewelry – pretty things, such as rings and necklaces, that you wear for decoration.

Ottoman Empire – a state founded by tribes in Turkey that ruled most of the land around the Mediterranean Sea in the 1500s and 1600s.

overlap – to lie partly on top of something.

permission – when a person in charge says it's okay to do something.

strap – a strip of leather, cloth, or plastic that keeps something tied on.

swirl – to whirl or to move smoothly in circles.

tradition – a belief or practice passed through a family or group of people.